WORLD SOCCER CLUBS

REAL MADRID

by Derek Moon

Copyright © 2025 by Press Room Editions. All rights reserved. No part of this book may be used or reproduced in any manner whatsoever, including internet usage, without written permission from the copyright owner, except in the case of brief quotations embodied in critical articles and reviews.

Book design by Kate Liestman
Cover design by Kate Liestman

Photographs ©: Fernando Pidal/SOPA Images/Sipa USA/AP Images, cover; Diego Souto/Quality Sport Images/Getty Images Sport/Getty Images, 5; David S. Bustamante/Soccrates Images/Getty Images Sport/Getty Images, 7; Julian Finney/Getty Images Sport/Getty Images, 9; Gianni Ferrari/Cover/Getty Images, 11, 15; AP Images, 13; Central Press/Hulton Archive/Getty Images, 17; Etsuo Hara/Getty Images Sport/Getty Images, 19; Shaun Botterill/Getty Images Sport/Getty Images, 21, 25; Manuel Blondeau/AOP.Press/Corbis Sport/Getty Images, 23; Alvaro Medranda/Quality Sport Images/Getty Images Sport/Getty Images, 27; Denis Doyle/Getty Images Sport/Getty Images, 29

Press Box Books, an imprint of Press Room Editions.

ISBN
978-1-63494-962-0 (library bound)
978-1-63494-976-7 (paperback)
979-8-89469-007-0 (epub)
978-1-63494-990-3 (hosted ebook)

Library of Congress Control Number: 2024940871

Distributed by North Star Editions, Inc.
2297 Waters Drive
Mendota Heights, MN 55120
www.northstareditions.com

Printed in the United States of America
012025

ABOUT THE AUTHOR

Derek Moon is an author who lives in Watertown, Massachusetts, with his wife and daughter.

TABLE OF CONTENTS

CHAPTER 1
KINGS OF EUROPE 4

CHAPTER 2
BECOMING REAL 10

CHAPTER 3
A TEAM OF STARS 16

CHAPTER 4
A HIGHER LEVEL 22

SUPERSTAR PROFILE
CRISTIANO RONALDO 28

QUICK STATS 30
GLOSSARY 31
TO LEARN MORE 32
INDEX 32

CHAPTER 1

KINGS OF EUROPE

Time was running out on Real Madrid in the 2022 Champions League. The Spanish power had reached the round of 16. But Madrid lost 1–0 to Paris Saint-Germain (PSG) in the first game. Then in the second game, PSG went up 1–0 in the 39th minute. That meant Madrid needed two goals just

Karim Benzema scored 15 goals in 12 Champions League games during the 2021–22 season.

to tie the series. Madrid striker Karim Benzema didn't panic.

Real Madrid is the most successful team in Spain. No team has won more championships in La Liga, the country's top league. *Los Blancos* (The Whites) have shined even brighter in Europe. Madrid always seemed capable of magic in the Champions League. Never was that truer than in 2022.

Benzema scored a hat trick in the second half against PSG. That gave Madrid a 3–2 win in the series. And the team's magic was only beginning. Next came Chelsea in the quarterfinals. Los Blancos once again trailed late. Winger Rodrygo tied the series in the 80th minute.

Rodrygo (21) connects with a header against Manchester City in the 2022 Champions League semifinal.

Then Benzema completed the comeback in extra time.

Los Blancos faced an even harder test in the semifinal. Through 89 minutes in the second game, Manchester City led 5–3. But Rodrygo needed only two minutes to tie the series. And once again,

Benzema clinched the win in extra time. Madrid was headed to the final after another comeback.

A strong Liverpool team awaited. Liverpool created many scoring chances. However, Los Blancos eventually took control. In the 59th minute, Federico Valverde found space on the right wing. He drove a low cross into the penalty area. An open Vinícius Júnior thumped it

SAVE MACHINE

Thibaut Courtois anchored Real Madrid's run to the 2022 European title. The goalkeeper was at his best in the final. He made nine saves and kept Liverpool from scoring in that game. No goalie has ever stopped more shots in a Champions League final.

Real Madrid celebrates winning the 2022 Champions League title.

into the goal. No comeback was needed this time. Madrid held on for a 1–0 win. Los Blancos became champions of Europe once again. And with 14 titles, they now had twice as many as the next best team.

CHAPTER 2

BECOMING REAL

Soccer arrived in Spain during the late 1800s. Real Madrid formed in 1902. The team has worn its famous all-white uniforms from the beginning. Early on, the team was known as Madrid Football Club. In 1920, King Alfonso XIII awarded the club the title *Real* (Royal). The team has been named Real Madrid ever since.

Ignacio Zoco shows off Real Madrid's all-white uniform before a game in 1964.

Madrid enjoyed some early success. In 1903, the team helped create the tournament now known as the Copa del Rey. That is the top cup tournament in Spain. Los Blancos won it in 1905. Then they also won the next three. La Liga began in 1929. Madrid claimed its first title in 1932.

EL CLÁSICO

In the 1950s, forward Alfredo Di Stéfano agreed to join Barcelona. Then he signed with Real Madrid instead. The move helped ignite one of soccer's greatest rivalries. Barcelona and Real Madrid are now two of the sport's most successful clubs. Each team represents opposing regions in Spain. Their meetings are nicknamed *El Clásico* (The Classic).

Alfredo Di Stéfano (far right) scored 227 goals in 11 seasons with Real Madrid.

Real Madrid only got better in the 1950s. Alfredo Di Stéfano led the way. The talented forward joined the club in 1953. Los Blancos won La Liga titles in 1954 and 1955. Then they took over Europe.

The European Cup began in 1956. The top clubs in Europe played one another to crown the best team on the continent. Behind Di Stéfano, Madrid reached the 1956 final. Los Blancos gave up two goals in the first 10 minutes. But Madrid staged a comeback to win 4–3. That began Madrid's success in the tournament.
Los Blancos went on to win the first five European titles. The tournament has since become known as the Champions League. Madrid remains the only team to have won it five years in a row.

The club boasted talent all over the field. In 1958, Ferenc Puskás arrived. He paired with Di Stéfano to create one of the best forward lines in soccer history.

Real Madrid players walk with the European Cup trophy after winning the tournament in 1960.

The duo put on a show in the 1960 European Cup final. Madrid won the game 7–3. Di Stéfano scored a hat trick. Puskás netted the other four.

CHAPTER 3

A TEAM OF STARS

Real Madrid didn't slow down in the 1960s. Ferenc Puskás scored 28 La Liga goals in the 1960–61 season. Alfredo Di Stéfano added 21 more. Real Madrid dominated Spanish soccer over the next nine seasons. The team won La Liga eight times. Only in 1966 did Los Blancos fall short. But they won another European Cup that year.

Ferenc Puskás scored 242 goals in 262 games for Real Madrid.

Madrid enjoyed periods of greatness in the following years. Beginning in 1975, the team won La Liga five times in six seasons. Then it won five league titles in a row during the late 1980s. However, the team struggled to break through in Europe. Then in the 1990s, Barcelona became the best team in La Liga.

Raúl debuted for Madrid in 1994. The forward was only 17 years old. He would go on to play a record 741 games for Los Blancos. During that time, he scored 323 goals. Raúl also helped push Madrid back to the top of Europe.

Madrid reached the Champions League final in 1998. A powerful Juventus squad awaited. Forward Predrag Mijatović scored

Predrag Mijatović (center) scored only one goal during the 1997–98 Champions League, but it came in the final.

the game's only goal. That lifted Madrid to its first European title in 32 years. Two years later, Madrid made it back to the final. Raúl scored a goal in a 3–0 win.

That summer, Florentino Pérez took over as Madrid's president. The team already had big stars. However, Pérez wanted to sign more. In a shocking move, he brought in midfielder Luís Figo from Barcelona. Zinedine Zidane, the former world player of the year, arrived the next summer. Because of its many stars, Madrid became known as the *Galácticos* (Galactics, or Superstars).

The talented squad won another Champions League title in 2002. However,

POLITICAL TIES

Dictator Francisco Franco ruled Spain from 1939 until 1975. Real Madrid became his favorite team. Los Blancos came to unofficially represent his government. This increased tension with Barcelona, where the local Catalan people sought to leave Spain. Today, Franco and his dictatorship are gone. Even so, Real Madrid is still seen as the team of Spain's political establishment.

Zinedine Zidane (in white) avoids a defender during a Champions League game in 2003.

that proved to be the high point of this era. Ronaldo and David Beckham soon added more star power. But the Galácticos experiment didn't go as planned. Pérez stepped down in 2006 after three seasons without another major trophy.

CHAPTER 4

A HIGHER LEVEL

Florentino Pérez returned in 2009 to try again. Real Madrid already had a great goalie in Iker Casillas. And Sergio Ramos was a world-class defender. In 2009, the team brought in attackers Cristiano Ronaldo and Kaká. Both had been the world player of the year before. Talented striker Karim Benzema arrived, too. The next summer, Madrid

Iker Casillas played 725 games for Real Madrid.

hired José Mourinho. Now the team had a star manager.

All the big moves paid off. In the past, Mourinho had often used a defensive strategy. However, the 2011–12 Madrid squad focused on offense. Los Blancos scored 121 goals. That broke the La Liga record by 14. Ronaldo scored 46 of those goals.

Winning the Champions League again became Madrid's top priority. Mourinho was gone by 2013. But the star players kept coming. In 2014, Los Blancos faced neighbors Atlético Madrid in the Champions League final. Atlético took an early lead. The game remained 1–0 through 90 minutes. However, Ramos

In 2016, Sergio Ramos became the first defender to score in two Champions League finals.

tied it in stoppage time. Then Real scored three goals in extra time to win 4–1.

Two years later, the same teams met again in the final. Los Blancos won in a shootout. Then they beat Juventus and

Liverpool in the next two finals. Real Madrid became the first team to win three straight European titles since 1976.

Ronaldo left after the three-peat. Madrid quickly reloaded. Luka Modrić continued to control the midfield. Vinícius Júnior developed into one of the world's best forwards. His goal against Liverpool in 2022 helped Madrid win the European title. Soon, midfielder Jude Bellingham

SANTIAGO BERNABÉU

Real Madrid has played in the Santiago Bernabéu since 1947. The massive stadium is one of the most famous in the world. It is named after the club's former president. In 2019, Madrid began a major renovation. The updates included adding a retractable roof.

In 2024, Luka Modrić won his sixth Champions League title with Real Madrid.

joined Los Blancos. In 2024, he lifted Madrid to its 15th Champions League title. Europe's most successful team showed no signs of slowing down.

SUPERSTAR PROFILE

CRISTIANO RONALDO

Cristiano Ronaldo rose to stardom with Manchester United. In 2009, Real Madrid came calling. The team offered $131.5 million for him. That was a huge price at the time. The Portuguese forward proved to be worth every penny.

Ronaldo had won the 2008 Ballon d'Or. That trophy is awarded to the world's best player each year. He won four more with Madrid. Scoring became routine for Ronaldo. Over nine seasons with Madrid, he scored 451 times. That set a team record. Ronaldo averaged more than one goal per game. His scoring led Madrid to massive success. Los Blancos won La Liga twice with Ronaldo. They also won the Champions League four times.

Ronaldo also brought new life to El Clásico. Lionel Messi had turned Barcelona into a superpower. Meanwhile, Ronaldo helped Madrid return to the top. The two players were all-time greats. Their meetings in El Clásico became must-see events.

Cristiano Ronaldo scored a career-high 48 La Liga goals during the 2014–15 season.

QUICK STATS

REAL MADRID

Founded: 1902

Home stadium: Santiago Bernabéu

La Liga titles: 36

European Cup/Champions League titles: 15

Copa del Rey titles: 20

Key managers:

- Miguel Muñoz (1959, 1960–74): 9 La Liga titles, 2 European Cup titles, 3 Copa del Rey titles

- Vicente del Bosque (1994, 1996, 1999–2003): 2 La Liga titles, 2 Champions League titles

- Zinedine Zidane (2016–18, 2019–21): 2 La Liga titles, 3 Champions League titles

Most career appearances: Raúl (741)

Most career goals: Cristiano Ronaldo (451)

Stats are accurate through the 2023–24 season.

GLOSSARY

debuted
Made a first appearance.

dictator
A leader with absolute power, especially one who uses that power in a cruel way.

era
A period of time in history.

establishment
A group of people who form a ruling class.

extra time
Two 15-minute halves that take place if a knockout game is tied after 90 minutes of play.

hat trick
When a player scores three or more goals in a game.

penalty area
The 18-yard box in front of the goal where a player is granted a penalty kick if he or she is fouled.

rivalries
Ongoing competitions that bring out the greatest emotion from fans and players.

shootout
A way of deciding a tie game. Players from each team take a series of penalty kicks.

stoppage time
Time added to the end of a soccer match to account for stoppages in play.

TO LEARN MORE

Hewson, Anthony K. *GOATs of Soccer*. North Mankato, MN: Abdo Publishing, 2022.

Marthaler, Jon. *The Best Teams of World Soccer*. Minneapolis: Abdo Publishing, 2024.

Streeter, Anthony. *World Cup All-Time Greats*. Mendota Heights, MN: Press Box Books, 2024.

MORE INFORMATION

To learn more about Real Madrid, go to **pressboxbooks.com/AllAccess**. These links are routinely monitored and updated to provide the most current information available.

INDEX

Beckham, David, 21
Bellingham, Jude, 26
Benzema, Karim, 6–8, 22

Casillas, Iker, 22
Courtois, Thibaut, 8

Di Stéfano, Alfredo 12–15, 16

Figo, Luís, 20

Júnior, Vinícius, 8, 26

Kaká, 22

Messi, Lionel, 28
Mijatović, Predrag, 18
Modrić, Luka, 26
Mourinho, José, 24

Pérez, Florentino, 19–21, 22
Puskás, Ferenc, 14–15, 16

Ramos, Sergio, 22, 24
Raúl, 18–19
Rodrygo, 6–7
Ronaldo, 21
Ronaldo, Cristiano, 22, 24, 26, 28

Valverde, Federico, 8

Zidane, Zinedine, 20